# *Golfing with the Angels*

*A How-to Guide to Navigate Your Game & Life*

Denise Kane

**Violet Star Press**

The characters and events portrayed in this book are fictitious. Any similarity to real persons, living or dead, is coincidental and not intended by the author.



ISBN-13: 979-8-9991972-0-7 (paperback)
ISBN-13: 979-8-9991972-1-4 (eBook)

Cover design by: Billy Design
Library of Congress Control Number: TXu 2-057-437
Printed in the United States of America

*The guidance from all of us angels is as simple and complex as life: ask for and trust the Divine help you get, have fun, and be courageous when you're called to do something important. That's the point of it all, anyway.*

GOLFING ANGELS

# Contents

# Preface

After a career with American Airlines for thirty-eight years, I passionately embraced my spiritual journey, and a life-changing, jaw-dropping experience convinced me to uproot my life of corporate employee to follow a guided calling toward golf—*a sport I recently became interested in*—so that I could play my role in bringing the power of the angels to the mainstream.

# Prologue

Success during a game of golf most certainly starts—and ends—in the mind. It's a series of focused steps involving calculated decision-making, measuring, correcting, and overcorrecting. But as with every other sport, the game should bring you joy. Too often, golfers give the impression they're taking themselves far too seriously.

Whether you're a pro, a driving machine, a hacker, a weekend warrior, or someone in between, every round depends on the player's state of mind. Almost all that tension can be eased with the right guidance. Some athletes rely solely on their coaches or a player they aspire to be more like ... but every golfer has far more support than he or she could ever dream of.

*Golfing with the Angels* clarifies how even athletes have dedicated angels who want to help them experience their sport with more fun, joy and success. It divulges how to benefit from the angels *inside information* and help from their *birds'-eye view* will not only change the readers' game, but it'll change their lives.

# Introduction: The Starter

I've always been an athlete, and until 2005 I skied semi-competitively while I worked at American Airlines. But once I discovered golf, it consumed me. I uprooted my whole life to pursue this new passion—sold my condo, went part-time with the airlines, and devoted my spare time to golf lessons, being diligent about my learning until it was *finally as fun as I knew it could be.*

What excited me the most about the sport was that I could see it would challenge me until my last breath, and that kind of challenge had been missing in my life. I had always wanted to find my passion. This newfound hobby gave me that.

In 2006, I'd been playing golf for about six years when a coworker with whom I'd never spoken and knew only from large-scale company meetings experienced inconsolable tragedy: his 24 year-old son died in a terrible car wreck.

One afternoon about six months after that death, I stood in my kitchen, making a cheesecake. My mind was quiet, tranquil, at peace. Penetrating that stillness, I heard a voice.

"Hi, I'm Thomas Keys ... I need you to tell my dad that I'm fine, that it wasn't painful, and I'm good. Over here everything is great."

This single moment changed my world view and redirected my life.

First off, stunned doesn't begin to cover what I felt. To explain what happened next, let me backtrack to say that my mom had been deceased for a little over a year. We'd been extremely close. And after she passed over, the same thing had happened, except not verbally. At times, I'd intuitively sensed her presence in the room and by seeing flashes of light. I would feel her touch me on the face, sit on my bed before falling asleep (that was creepy the first time), and fix the front of my hair (as she would do when alive) as I was going out the door. Once when I was at the gym, sitting on a yoga mat in front of the mirror, doing a side stretch, I looked into the mirror; my mom's face was superimposed on mine. Yup, and another instance, when I got my driver's license renewed and the clerk handed me my new license, my mom's face was looking back at me. I blinked my eyes in disbelief, staring at her picture, which soon faded and my image appeared. However, the very first time she communicated with me shortly after her passing was through a song.

I was perplexed about how to word the sentiment on her memorial plate. Besides her name, birth and death date, there was a space for a few memorable words. I wanted it to be special and unique. The others in the mausoleum read *Wonderful Wife & Mother, Outstanding Cook,* etc., but that wasn't resonating with me. One morning about a month after her passing, I woke up singing the song "Forever Young" by Rod Stewart. It took a few minutes for this realization to set in, and when it did I knew it was the answer to my prayers. What a relief!

She was a meticulous shopper and to this day is my go-to angel for help in finding a sassy outfit or a reliable repairman. My mom continues to communicate with me regularly through songs, through others by overhearing their conversations, and by answering my varied requests for advice on things little and big. I knew that wherever she was she would answer my call. Just knew it.

When I received the message from Thomas, I had a choice. I could have acted or not acted on that impulse. Taking the message to his dad redirected my life. It revealed to me there's so much we don't understand, especially about death. Everything I thought I knew came undone, and I viewed the world, my circumstances, and life from a different perspective.

Why was I the recipient of the message? As I concluded, I was in a creative-meditative space while I was baking—my mind was receptive to the impulse, which flowed clearly. When this occurred, I stopped what I was doing, stepped back, and thought, *that was bizarre.* With certainty, I knew those weren't my words and that they had to come from an outside energy. *How could this be? I didn't even know him. Why would he choose me? How am I going to get the message to his dad? There's no way I'm going to do this.* But somewhere deep down inside, I knew I had to. My palms were sweating.

A week or so later, my mom came through intuitively with the suggestion of making her signature dish, pot roast, and taking a sandwich to his dad, which I did, and it worked out miraculously. This despite the fact that I thought, *How the heck am I going to find him in another department at the airport, I'll be out of my work area, what will I say, he'll think I'm crazy....* You get the gist! Well, the Universe made it happen effortlessly.

I devised a plan: get to work early before my schedule shift, bring the pot roast sandwich and carry in my arms a ream of white printer paper as a decoy. The paper decoy was in case anyone asked why I was out of my work area; I would tell them the pilot's briefing room needed paper. I hid the sandwich with the paper and proceeded with all the courage I could muster. The pilot's briefing room is a small 12' by 12' room with two doors, one leading to the main hallway and one into the break room for the ramp employees. As I entered the room from the hallway, Tommy was entering from the break room. I caught my breath in amazement.

Somehow I managed to utter a "hi" and a sentiment and give him a hug, and then said, "I have a pot roast sandwich for you."

He surprisingly said, "You do!"

I then blurted out, "Oh, and by the way, your son spoke to me; he's fine, all is well, and it wasn't painful."

By now I was in a full-body sweat in my wool

polyester uniform. What most astounded me was Tommy's response.

"Thank you. I appreciate you letting me know." At first, he appeared stunned by the stream of words pouring out of me, but then his face relaxed and a look of relief washed over him.

I was relieved and able to take a deep breath. I didn't stay to say anything more. I was just grateful to have managed to get it said. When I returned to my break room, which was surprisingly empty, on the table was the obituary of Thomas from the newspaper which was posted on our bulletin board six months earlier. I knew instantly this was a message thanking me. Tears welled up in my eyes and I realized something special just happened.

Taken together, the two events jolted me into realizing there would never be enough time in this life to do all the wonderful things we want to—even if we live healthily into our hundreds!

I woke up, as the saying goes, which coincided with turning 50 years old. Instantly, continuing over the next months, I dove into exploring angels, chakras, and energy healing. But what most intrigued me was the work of two powerful authors: Sonia Choquette and Doreen Virtue. To give only the briefest introduction, Sonia is a *New York Times* bestselling author and spiritual teacher who highlights the sixth sense; Doreen, "the Angel Lady," is an international bestselling author, a doctor of psychology, and a born clairvoyant. I fervently delved into their books and participated in in-person workshops by both Sonia and Doreen. Their books and workshops taught me about the angelic realm and how to enlist and call upon the angels for the big and small things in life.

Embracing the angels and their guidance incredibly changed how I viewed the world. It affirmed I'm not alone on this journey *(on and off the golf course!)*—far from it. I'm always loved and supported by these compassionate beings. My new outlook revamped my life: I had been a corporate executive working for the airlines; in little more than the blink of an eye, here I was on a totally different path, following a guided calling toward golf, determined to play my role in bringing the power of the angels to the mainstream.

I envision this book as taking off in a way that it becomes part one of a series, much in the same way the *For Dummies* books work but instead for sports and angels, starting with the sport closest to my heart: golf.

In the four years since my first contact with a spirit other than my mother, I began to experience various signs I interpreted as spirit guide and angelic presence. For instance, I would get chills, hear buzzing in my ears, see sparks of light in the daytime, or at night view a whole kaleidoscope of light which would wake me up. I discovered I was actually a medium. This discovery came about primarily by opening myself up to a wealth of guidance. I would ask for a parking spot, and someone would be backing out. Of course, part of me thought: *It's a coincidence.* But these coincidences kept happening. My shift in consciousness wasn't propelled by a dramatic moment other than as described. I would ask my team of angels in the morning for help in the day, and to clear the highways and byways on my commute. One day I entered the busy Interstate-540 at the noontime rush period, and there were literally no cars. Not one. I thought the roads might be closed, which was not the case; such incidents often felt numinous and continue to this day. I said to the angels, *It must be quite an undertaking to clear I-540, but it's a lot of fun.*

I had never "seen" the angels but knew they

were on the job because of the many synchronicities whenever I called on them. Other examples: All the signal lights were magically green as I made my way to an appointment that I was running late for. Or when I had only ten minutes to spare and quickly dashed into the store to find the perfect top for my fiftieth birthday celebration at an unbelievable price.

After a while, I became confident enough to come *out of the closet* and decided to use the "A" word at work. Soon after the moment of the spirit contact in the kitchen and lasting the final seven years of my career with American Airlines, during which I oversaw the operation of many departments, there were many times an employee needed help with a task, and I would say, "I'll call the angels." Sure enough, my coworkers welcomed the assistance without a smirk or *deer in the headlights* stare. I've even mentioned the angels when assisting passengers (total strangers) when I got fearless. To this day, no one has ever responded negatively.

One day I saw the engine of a plane being worked on by the mechanics. An employee came running up to me and said, "The plane is broken. Call the angels." He said this right in front of a passenger. I said, "I already did." In two minutes the plane was up and running.

And then there was the time at work after a plea, the angels fixed a mechanical problem, which was supposedly unfixable, in a jiffy. Our mechanics are top notch and the best in the business although at times, if a system of the aircraft won't work properly, the mechanics are required to put the aircraft out of service. That's where a dose of angel magic comes in to miraculously fix the issue.

After four years of using the angels' help, I took workshops on channeling, nature spirits, developing intuition, energy healing, and deeper study of the angelic realm. Up to this point, I had never encountered them on the golf course. That was all about to change.

Since I was already getting the angels' help and advice on everything from parking spots to sales on slacks, why not during my round (i.e., eighteen holes)? In hindsight, I'm not sure now why it took me four years, until August 2010, to beckon their help. Initially, I asked them to help me *get the ball in the hole with the fewest shots*, which didn't work very well—the first time or on several occasions that followed. It took a while to fine-tune our communication skills, determining how they could assist best. Most of all, how they could convey messages to me via signs on the course, relaying their tips and two-cents. It took many shots and loads of patience on both our parts to devise a strategy, as the following pages demonstrate. As the material in this book unfolded through me during my rounds, I had to experience it, discern what happened, then write about it. Many times as I played a shot, I knew there was substantial evidence. Not until I wrote about it afterwards did I realize the message, which accounted for much head scratching and giggles.

Guidance comes in many forms, and one particular day early on—September 2010—it came in stereo. I told two friends I was now using the angels to help me in golf, and they simultaneously chorused, "You need to write a book," to which I remarked, "No, I don't think so." I was not a word person or even a book person, so why would God play such a trick by getting me, an athlete, bogged down writing when I could be skiing down a race course or walking up the hills of a golf course? That indeed reaffirms the Divine has a sense of humor.

Then the realization set in. I knew I was meant

to share my secret with the world and create this book. It details how to call, communicate with, and use the *Golfing Angels* to enhance your round and make it much *more* fun. The angels have simple tips and techniques to help with every aspect, as they are masters at reading the greens, discerning target lines, and providing guidance on club and shot selection amidst the myriad of choices. Plus, a whole gamut of variables like fortuitous bounces off trees, cart paths, and other hard objects; miracles—including your ball skipping on water more times than physics would allow—and magical moments. Just to name a few! Now, with my newfound conviction, I swing with confidence, knowing I have my Angel Caddies on the bag. This has made a huge difference in my game by eliminating second-guessing, anxiety, and negativity—well, most of the time, that is—and bolstering my love of the game.

It took a while for me to embrace full trust. Even to this day, I must admit I have occasional lapses. The angels have an array of anecdotes validating that trust is a tricky thing, which I'll share with you as the pages roll. I'll warn you, the angels are addictive, and once you begin interacting with them consciously, you'll never stop.

Not fully understanding how they can be of assistance or even believing in their existence, like me when I started out, you may be hesitant to call on the angels. I can assure you these powerful, benevolent beings are a special gift available to all. They always have your best interests at heart (even though it may not always appear that way) and will provide companionship, clarity, comfort, humor, and so much more. A term they didn't coin but apply a lot to themselves is providers of *inside information* —that is, access to all sorts of knowledge and data we couldn't ever imagine—and they're ready, waiting, *hoping* to assist you in ways you never thought possible. The angels want you to dream big, ask away, and most importantly have fun.

Over the years, I have refined the lines of communication with the Golfing Angels, so you'll be able to jump right in. Naturally, you'll find your own unique style of conversing. The best part of this unimaginable relationship is their playfulness. They've taught me to lighten up, especially during tournaments, to accept what is—*the good, the bad, and the bunkers (those pesky sand traps)*—and to make the best of *every* situation.

My hope is that with an open mind, you'll

more swiftly understand the angels and see their subtle signs for yourself; they love that my stories offer tangible proof. So much so that they insisted I let them convey the stories through *their* eyes and voices, and, when a chorus of angels insists, I listen!

# Believing

We are thrilled to be called upon and delighted to help you in every way throughout your round. From reading the greens to guiding you to take advantage of fortuitous bounces, our aim is to assist as you embrace more joy and ease. There's no longer any need to stress over a two-foot putt, with us on your bag. We've got a whole team of Angel Caddies ready to assist with *every* aspect of your round, if you so choose.

We're an enchanting bunch of benevolent beings with a sensational sense of humor. Our rates are reasonable; for payment we only request a sincere "thank you." With our inside information, and something we call our *bird's-eye view*, we know exactly what you need in every moment (even better than you do) to bring more enjoyment to your game. And best of all, we're at your beck and call, twenty-four seven. We're your Angel Caddies, super support team!

When Denise first called us to help with her golf game, we were elated. It's always a pleasure to be of service—we love helping humans lighten up. We quickly realized that even though the human objective seems to be a low score, the *real* objective is to have a great time. Denise reminded us that humans like to play sports to connect with their inner child, and to give them a well-needed break from the stresses of daily life. But we also learned about how satisfying it is to hit the sweet spot every now and then.

As we walked the course with Denise, we saw how to be of help by lining up putts, tee shots, and approach shots. Also how we could weave balls through trees with the greatest of ease, ping-ponging them out onto the fairway. It took time (and a light sense of humor) to develop clear and effective lines of communication, and oh, the stories! We hope you'll laugh in the same way we did as we tried to understand each other's needs and communicate them effectively.

Our Angel Caddie partnership with Denise has developed over many years, and she's had to learn much trust and faith. It isn't an easy thing to trust us impeccably, although at any time, Denise can disregard what we recommended. The most rewarding time for us is when she takes our advice, makes the putt, and then whispers, "Thank you, angels!" Woohoo!

We help whoever asks, simply because we want to—but not because we have to. It is our joy to be of service to the Creator by serving humanity, including you golfers, weekend warriors, and hackers, regardless of your religious dogma.

It is always your choice to call on us, and whether you use our input or not is entirely up to you. One day, you may only want to use us on putts; then another day, on club selection. Some days, you may not ask for our help at all, and other days you ask away. Since we don't have egos, we don't get offended. We patiently wait for your call, for serving you is our mission.

We can discern the direction of the grass that the human eye is unable to perceive and how the humidity, dew point, wind, and so on will affect the roll of the ball. At the human level, you are processing all the variables you know of through your mind, but we sense how the ball will react to *all* the variables—variables you wouldn't dream of considering! Also, since we have the scoop and are in the know—99 percent sure—we can make recommendations for compensations to your aim, direction, and even club selection.

There have been hundreds of times when Denise wondered why we aimed her left or guided her to use a club that—for a typical shot—she wouldn't normally use. Once she understood we are looking beyond the parameters of the single shot to the outcome, she trusted our adjustments.

For example, one day on the tee box, we lined her shot way left into the woods. She whispered, "You don't expect me to hit my ball into the woods!" and she realigned the tee shot to the left side of the fairway. The ball ended up in the right rough, so she instantly regretted her decision. It wasn't until she was walking to her ball, mentally replaying the tee box scenario, that she realized what we had been trying to tell her. It was an enlightening moment. *We* knew prior to her hitting her drive that she was going to push the ball right. If she had kept the line we gave her—aiming to the left woods—her shot would have landed in the middle of the fairway: her preshot intention. Though in the beginning she often mistrusted our guidance, she eventually got it (like you humans do!). It took only five years for her to have *almost* full trust—and some of you go whole lifetimes without it! So we think five years is pretty fantastic. We are continually amazed by you!

Once Denise realized we're *in the know* and privy to the outcome, it enhanced her trust and opened her up to limitless possibilities. She realized the next time something like this happened, she could aim for the woods, knowing she would push the shot or re-tee with a straighter line and make swing adjustments to *possibly* prevent a push (which is a ball flight to the right). She finds it advantageous to know in advance if she is going to mishit a shot, so we guide her to make a swing correction ... and most of the time she does. We love it when you trust us!

Part of the super support team includes Driving Angel Miss Daisy, who helps with a target line to insure a perfect angle for the second shot in; Angel Sandy ... any guesses? ... that's right, to extricate your ball from those nasty bunkers. Our newest member to the team is Ranger Angel Steve. Call on him to keep players ahead of you moving along at a nice pace. He'll also help your foursome locate balls that went astray. Putting Angel Pete is happy to help, for he has a keen eye and laser focus.

If you're still feeling skeptical about this whole angel thing, we understand. It is a stretch and a lot to wrap your mind around. Just for fun, pretend and embrace this concept. Imagine we are real, even if the thought *is* out of your comfort zone. Why? Believing helps makes it so, and we get a kick out of showing you one of the many mysteries in the world. We love interacting with humans, and we delight in flooding you with signs and messages—at times doing so through other humans, TV, music, and clouds to get our point across. Even if you doubt, we'll be there for you; all we require to communicate back to you is your permission. Unless you ask for help, our wings are tied (since you have free will and all!). Just know that we have unlimited minutes and free texting. We're just a "Help me, angels," away.

# Heavenly Lies: Harnessing Help

Your wish is our command ... yes, like the genie in the bottle. We can be of service in an array of ways, of course, as long as your request is not detrimental to yourself or others.

One way to harness us is on the tee box. Imagine you're on the tee box of hole #1, par 4, and you'd like your shot to be right of the 150-yard marker, since that will eliminate tree trouble on your second shot. We'll give you the perfect line for that to happen. How? Well, you'll stand behind the ball, and we'll have a leaf or old ball mark brought to your attention, twenty feet or so in front of *your* ball. When you place your ball on the tee, you will use this mark as your target. For additional assistance, you may even want to aim the line on the ball in the direction of this target.

Just as Denise did, at first, you may

think we are directionally challenged, but you're forgetting we have inside information. Trust us; we calculate the earth's rotation, barometric pressure, gravitational pull, geese contrails, and pollen count ... just to name a few—all the outside factors in concurrence. It's as simple as that!

Our messages are abounding and unceasing. Sometimes they come lickety-split, like in the following instance. Standing over the putt, Denise heard car brakes screeching in the distance in spite of this hole's lack of proximity to a street. She dropped the ball—so to speak—and missed our message prior to hitting the putt, which zoomed past the hole. In hindsight, she realized the message was to put on the brakes, to slow down the putt. Our messages can be disguised or distinct, hinging on your heedfulness.

The putting green is another place we excel. To determine the putting line, we suggest you stand behind the ball mark and look toward the cup to sense if the putt is breaking right or left, or you may find it beneficial to look at the hole from the other side. Once you've discerned which way the putt is breaking, ask us for assistance, then—depending on the break you identified—look either right or left of the hole. We'll point out a spot; for instance, a discoloration in the grass or an old ball mark. This is your putting line ... or, as we like to call it, the *sink line*. As you replace your ball on the green, align it with the *sink line* for added assistance, and you'll be surely sinkable.

We hear you asking, "What if the putt is straight?" On the blue moon chance that you encounter a straight putt, simply don't look for a sink line. And if you are unable to determine the break, do not worry. In these two situations, it's best to trust us. Call on Putting Angel Pete, take a deep breath, and place the line on the ball toward the hole without focusing too much on the hole. Trust us, breathe calmly, and let us guide your hand to line up the ball with the sink line. In the next chapter, we'll show you how we taught Denise our technique to determine the speed of the greens, which we call the *speed spot*. Are you hanging off the edge of your seat yet?

We had the most fun with Denise just the other day, when she was ready to putt. She had the line on the ball facing the sink line, but the ball would not stay still; it kept oscillating. She marked the ball and tried to line it up again, but it kept wobbling! Feeling rushed, she firmly placed the ball down, made the shot, and shaved the edge of the hole. Once she walked off the greens, the "aha" bells were going off like crazy: ding, ding, ding! We tried communicating that the sink line was wrong, so now Denise knows that oscillation means the sink line is askew. From there, she can ask for a new line with a slight adjustment. That's just one fun way we communicate! Sometimes you'll get it; sometimes you won't. But it won't stop our ding, ding, ding! There are no accidents, and everything is a message. Just as Denise has, you'll also get better with practice. Is that a bell I hear?

Often, it is easier for us to communicate through others by directing our messages through them. A playing partner may remark, "The greens are running slow," or "I had a lesson last week and didn't realize I was swaying in my turn," or "That wasn't enough club; the wind must be blowing stronger." If you're paying attention, you'll intuitively know that was exactly what you needed to hear.

Are you hearing "aha" bells? Remember, if it's brought to your attention, pay attention! But always use discernment.

Once, while Denise was watching an LPGA (Ladies Professional Golfing Association) event, the announcer made a comment about Michelle Wie's new putting stroke, implying that she had been missing close putts because her eyes needed to be inside the ball. Denise had experienced that very problem that week; on hearing the announcer's comment, she sat up straight, listening intently. We *know* she got the memo for the next time she played!

One occasion, we plummeted a bale of pine needles to get her attention, just to remind her to lighten up and have fun—which she did! Often during tournaments she's very serious, which defeats the whole purpose of the game. Sometimes, as she addresses the ball, a ring tone may even bring forth a just-what-I-needed-to-hear message, such as "Hit Me with Your Best Shot" or "No Hook" or maybe "Slice." So we switch up our communication styles, which are endless!

Miracles are called for on certain shots. On one hole #8, for example, her second shot was on a steep side hill in the rough, and she had to cross a small stream in front of the green; she figured a miracle would be a good thing to ask for. Did we mention that your miracle account is infinite? Denise knows this, though she sometimes thinks there is a limited supply. The shot she hit was made for the ESPN highlight reel; it pared the hole. She was so proud ... and so were we!

Then another day, for her second shot into the green we had Denise pull a 9 iron. Even with the wind behind her, she questioned the suggestion, but she did surrender to it. Just as she addressed the ball, the wind gusts came on strong! As she swung, the wind howled and almost knocked her over, making her see why we had her choose a 9. Ding, ding, ding!

The wind is fun to play with, and we enormously enjoy swirling, gusting, and dancing it. Once, with a stiff breeze into Denise on the tee box of a par 3, she backed off the shot, reconsidering our club selection, and as she did, the wind stopped blowing completely. She chuckled to herself, realizing we had it all perfectly orchestrated. This daily test in trust keeps her sharp. One day on the tenth green, we indicated a leaf (one of the many) as her *sink line* (putting line). As she lined up, a big gust of wind blew all the leaves, except the target leaf. A few holes later, Denise had a lengthy putt and was picking the leaves off the *sink line*, when she realized a call to us for help might be beneficial. We immediately conjured up a hefty gust, which cleared the sink line. She should have asked sooner.

We love having onboard Atomic, the Physicist Angel, who adds a quantum level of physics to the game for us here in the angelic realm. Just the other day, Denise's tee shot came to rest with the line on the ball pointing to the green—in fact, to the pin, that is the flagstick marking the hole—and with the second shot it would end well past the pond. Her initial response was *how amazing is this* (by the way, we were delighted she noticed!) *that the line on her ball lined up to the pin!*

Then the doubt set in.

By using our alignment, she would have to hit a *perfect* iron out of the rough. So she opted to aim a little right, which took part of the largest section of the pond out of play, giving her a hill as backstop behind the green. Well, you know what happened. She hit a pure iron shot, and because she disregarded our line, she was short of the green on the fringe. Any other time she would have been thrilled, but when she realized the precise calculations we made to plan for the tee shot to stop at a position where the line on the ball pointed to the pin, she was disappointed. She said, "Never again … I trust the angels and my golf swing completely." If it could *only* be that easy!

We utterly understand what a big challenge it is to have trust and faith. It's certainly the biggest one for Denise. Even though she asks for our assistance, there is still an "I want to do it my way" attitude *sometimes,* and *sometimes* she even takes that route. Just recently she asked for club selection on a par 3; we recommended a 7 iron. Boldly, she told us, "I realize a 7 is probably the correct club, but I really want to hit my 8 iron." So she did, and her ball landed fifteen yards short of the pin. When she saw it, she remarked, “I knew you were right! I just wanted to prove it.”

Oh, the human dilemma!

# Seeing Is Believing

You may imagine us in a variety of ways, from fat babies with wings, to angelic-like beings you see in books, or maybe humanlike caddies, or even orbs of light. Whatever way you decide to visualize us is fine. Let your imagination soar! The sky's the limit!

Denise's first imagining of us is quite graphic. In her mind's eye, she had pictured five or six of us huddled around a tiny old black-and-white TV, with baseball caps and visors on, looking a tad bit disheveled. We would also be smoking what looked to be a cigar, but was something like kale or wheat germ. This first visualization happened several years after our initial encounters with her (triggered by attending workshops and reading angel books) but shortly after we started helping her with golf. One day, on the tee box of hole #16, she had a vision. She was in the middle of her backswing, and by mistake Putting Angel Pete's wing hit the "live feed button," which turned on the visual cortex in Denise's mind so that she actually saw us huddled around the small black-and-white TV in her inner vision. Well, with that minor interruption, which she thought was as good an excuse as any for the mishit, she pulled the shot left into a small grove of pine trees. We made sure she had a good lie on the pine straw, with an opening through the trees. It's the least we could do. She easily got out and recovered nicely, other than scratching her head.

Shortly after this episode, her imagination went further. In this more elaborate depiction, we follow her game from a NASA-like circular control room, with huge video monitors around the entire space. It's a whopping 360 degrees to oversee the course and have an eagle eye on all the comings and goings of the growing grass, the sun's angle, the geese, and Denise. There are three-tiered levels, with the "in charge" Golfing Angel on the top level in the center, hooked up with a Bluetooth-like device to communicate with Denise on the course. Needless to say, she was very impressed. We're up on all the latest technology and gadgetry. We're even able to move clouds, with the cloud-o-mover, to cover the green, thereby adjusting the roll of the green to make sure the putt is sunk, as well as increase the dew point, with the dew-ometer so her incoming shot onto the green will have less or more roll ... whatever is needed. We have it covered from top to bottom and from tee to green! Here, in her own words, is how we astounded Denise one day with our signs:

> Serendipitous signs are everywhere. Like today, when looking over my chip shot on the second hole for a target line, there was not one to be found. The greens were immaculate and shining in the early-morning November sun. As I stood behind the ball, I asked the angels for a target line, and sure enough, as if on cue from the Universe, a leaf-like helicopter thing, glided ever so gently while twirling in the breeze, landing ten feet in front of the ball. It seemed as if I was on a Hollywood set and the director called for action. This turned out to be the perfect target line, which left me a tap-in putt. The angels have impeccable timing and a whole repertoire of doohickeys, gizmos, and leaf-like things up their wings ... like Hermione's beaded handbag in Harry Potter.

One of Denise's golf buddies calls her daddy,

who is deceased, to help whenever her ball is heading for the tree. And without fail, her ball ever so gently falls out of the trees into the fairway. Sometimes when her ball is heading for the trees, the foursome will call out, "Daddy!"

The team of Golfing Angels may include those who while in physical form helped you love the game and now assist on the Angel Caddie team. We've got quite an array of expertise and experience.

Astonishing!

Just recently while watching an LPGA match on TV, Denise realized all the golfers had caddies by their side; she wondered why she didn't. Walking down the first fairway the next time she played, she asked for an on-course caddie. We jubilantly sent her Cliff. He'd been on the Golfing Angels team for some time, but mostly behind the scenes ... until now! Cliff is eager to be walking the course and sharing our transmissions on the best plan of action for each and every shot. Having a Golfing Angel walking the walk —on the same level, so to speak—has considerably enhanced *hearing* our guidance, as well as afforded a more human aspect to us. Cliff has changed the way Denise communicates with us too. She now discusses the best action and hashes things out with him as they occur. It's in line with having a *real* caddie.

Now with Cliff by her side and a gaggle of Golfing Angels in the control room, Denise has the luxury of being fully plugged in as we monitor all the factors to insure a most superb round.

# Driving on the Range

It's also especially advantageous to call on us at the driving range and practice facility. We can assist you with focus and clear intentions, resulting in a beneficial boost to your confidence.

We can help line up your shots or help with your swing, stance, etc. You may get a nudge to stand closer to the ball, tighten your grip, shorten your backswing, or shift your weight. We even have a "Physical" Angel coach, Seymour, so if you feel or sense physical jabs or subtle adjustments to your stance, setup or alignment, know it is us, assisting with specific swing issues. You'll receive intuitive guidance most likely during a relatively introspective time, like before falling asleep or while hanging in the hammock or meditating. It's necessary to make room for our messages to occur, since they may seem subtle at first. We'll also turn up the volume on our communications so they're easier to understand. We're happy to oblige. Ask away!

Since you've already mastered the sink line, we'll get right to the technique for determining the speed and detecting your *speed spot*. First, you'll need to decide if the putt is uphill or downhill. Walking the line of the putt is sometimes helpful so you can feel it in your feet or scrutinize the topography for clues. Once we concur with you on this vital piece of information, we'll point out a spot either past or short of the hole. If the greens are running fast or the putt is downhill, the speed spot will be short of the hole; if the greens are slow, or the putt is uphill, the speed spot will be past the hole. Again, this spot may be a discoloration in the grass, a mark on the green, a leaf-like thing, or anything else brought to your attention. It may even be another player's ball or ball mark.

Always go with your first instinct, because getting the mind involved will nullify our communication. When you ascertain this key ingredient, laser in on the speed spot to gauge the distance, and putt away with conviction. With your sink line and speed spot skills you'll be unstoppable. This meritable technique also works on the course, of course!

Well, most of the time that is. When Denise

landed on the green in regulation and had a thirty-foot putt, she called for a miracle. The greens were stressed from the hot weather; thin and bare patches made them roll ragged. Hitting the ball firmer was typically a better choice with the rough ride. Her first putt ran past the hole, leaving a five footer, since she failed to notice the putt was downhill. Even with our precise speed spot, she ran it through the break and was now left with a three footer, which then lipped out, dancing frustratingly about the rim of the hole but failing to fall in.

With erratic greens it's more important than ever to discern if the putt is downhill or uphill, as unpredictable greens play havoc with feel, hence trust. We counseled Denise to calculate the sink line and speed spot from various directions to eliminate those nasty four putts.

Sometimes— knowing we will guide her hand accordingly—Denise doesn't even look for the sink line but instead places her ball down on the putting green with the line on the ball facing the hole or thereabouts. She has become much more trusting over the years and much better at deep breathing too. In for two, hold, out for two, hold!

We're also able to practice for you when you're not able to get to the range, since we now have simulators we received as gifts last holiday season. This has been advantageous by providing an understanding of the dynamics of physics and the physical body. Our equipment includes a helmet with sensors, which enables us to feel as if we have a body, so we can experience the sensation of swinging the club and hitting the sweet spot. It's similar to the simulators set up in your local golf stores to demo clubs. Our four simulators give us the luxury of playing courses all over the world as a foursome. This has given us the ability to practice when Denise can't and we're able to keep her game sharp and skills polished. She didn't believe this was imaginable, until one winter day, when the weather wasn't favorable to practice, she asked for assistance. The next time she played, her game was outstanding; needless to say, she was amazed. It's now a common routine for us to practice while she's writing this book or doing other fun things.

Just recently, Denise realized if we're able to practice on her behalf, we can certainly take lessons on her behalf. We eagerly called in the best golf instructor from galaxies away to help. When her irons weren't cooperating, we got her back on track without having to break a sweat, get a callus, or even buy a bucket.

You may be shaking your head, wondering how you can benefit. Well, we simply do an energy transfer. It's similar to downloading your computer with new information and upgrades. The practice and lessons we have integrated on your behalf are energetically transferred, so your swing will be polished and perfectly ready for short grass and greens.

When Denise recently got a hiccup with her driver, she called on us. Since some irritation was setting in, it became difficult to comprehend our guidance. After the round, she gave us permission to practice and take lessons to get her back on track. Even though we skillfully adjusted her swing, the next time she played she felt—to regain confidence —the need to hit a few on the range. During her practice, we sent some intuitive nudges regarding the setup as she took her swing, reminding her to accelerate through and finish the shoulder turn. Something she forgets every now and then. It's always gratifying for us to jog her memory.

Another day before Denise's round she planned to hit a few on the range to loosen up. After practicing putting and chipping for several minutes, she realized she'd be too rushed to make it over to the driving range. On the way to the first tee, she remembered she had asked us to practice for her the day before. Trusting this, she felt confident. Sure enough, her swing was solid during a ladies' league team event, which contributed to a fun day and a second-place finish. Not to mention a chip in, earning her more dough. Show us the money!

# In the Bag

All we need from you is to hear "hit the cart path," or "get through the trees" and we are on it. Since trees are—golfers sometimes say—90 percent air, all we do is weave the ball as if we were knitting. It's quite easy once you get the hang of it. Sometimes it may sound like we're playing ping-pong before the ball is tossed out. And we are! Cart paths are easy too; it only requires a consultation with Angel Atomic to compute the forward motion and direction for beneficial results. We work quickly. An instant should do!

We also have any array of other fortuitous-bounce options at your disposal, like skipping on water or ricocheting off rocks, turtles' backs, carts, and trees. It's all in one simple call prior to play to give us the freedom to help you in multitudinous ways throughout your round. We'll arrange heaven-sent bounces and other lucky results.

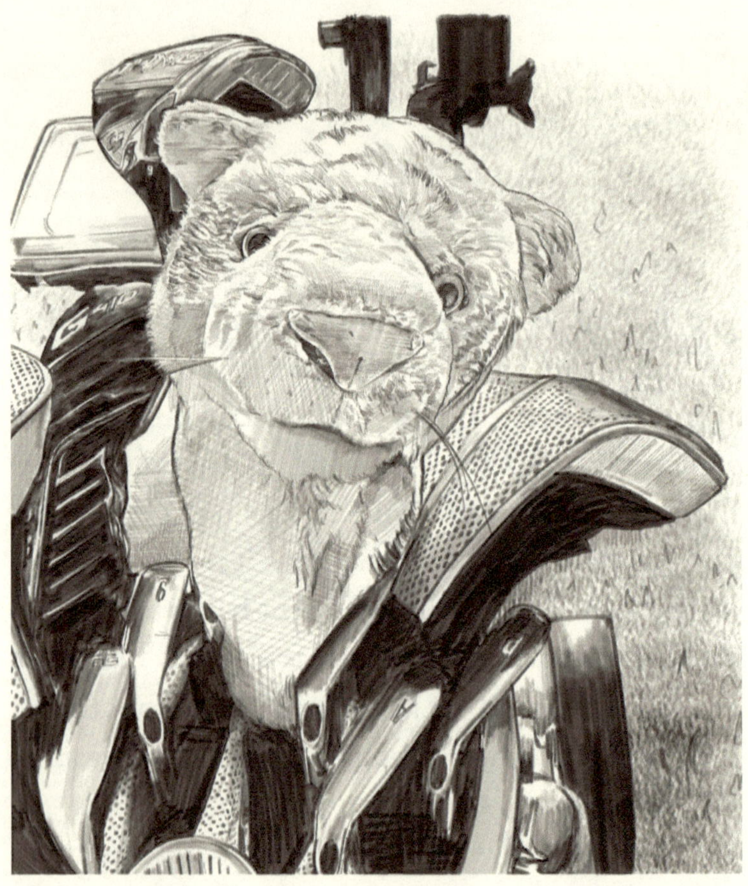

It wasn't until the third year of working with us that Denise realized we could help with club selection. That took a bit of getting used to, since she had to trust us even more. She was so conditioned to pick the club that it took time to work us seamlessly into her routine. Once she did, however, watch out!

She is certainly enjoying the luxury of having our expertise confirm the club, giving her the freedom to be relaxed and confident—not needing to mess around with any GPS gizmo or grass throwing.

Picking the correct club is a straightforward matter with us. When Denise gets to her ball, she gets a sense of what club she would select. Then we confirm. For example, she is feeling a 6 iron for a certain shot. She'll ask us if this is correct and will sense a yes or no in her mind's eye. If she gets a no, she will then ask, is a 5 iron the correct club and so on until she gets a yes. It's typically not a long or tedious process. She usually gets it right the first time. Bravo!

Lately, after being assisted with club selection for many years, she now walks up to her ball and sees a number or letter in her mind's eye, which may be a 6 or a 9, or a P (pitching wedge) or an A (wedge). Certainly when she sees a 5 or a 7, she knows the difference in a 5 iron over a 5 wood and a 7 wood over a 7 iron. It's that simple—once you have trust, that is. And now with caddie Cliff on her bag, if she is indecisive, they can toss around options until confidence is anchored.

One round, she was hitting all her clubs well although she opted to use one more club than our guidance. Two shots were over water and one over a minefield of bunkers in front of the green. For obvious reasons, she was more comfortable having more club than less. We're cool with that! She pared the holes with no harm done, *except it negated the birdies we had planned.* She was happy with the pars, and that's all that matters.

Just recently, as she approaches the ball, she has begun to sense the club we are mentally suggesting. She may be walking down the fairway one hundred yards from her ball and already sees in her mind's eye what club we are recommending. Whether or not she takes our *words of wisdom* is another story. *Que sera sera*!

Okay, so you're saying what is this mind's eye thing? Well, it's the human's ability to visualize mental images ... like daydreaming. Say, we told you to imagine yourself at the beach, sitting in a chair and looking at the ocean. You could easily do this with your eyes open or closed. You are seeing the ocean in your mind's eye. This "seeing" happens in the space between your two physical eyes. The more you play with your imagination, the clearer and stronger it gets. You may be thinking: *There is no way I can do this*. Believe us, you can! Practice makes perfect ... like the golf swing.

During a recent round, for the second shot on a par 4 we sent her the image of a P, for her pitching wedge; inadvertently, she pulled her 9 iron. When she got home, she replayed the hole in her mind and wondered why the shot went long. Then the light went on! She saw the P in the mind's eye, but reversed it as a mirror image and pulled the 9. There's a first time for everything! The good news is these are the only two clubs that would allow this mix-up to occur.

Another time, on an uphill par 3 the pin was forward. Denise's first instinct was to use a 5 iron; however, with our *inside information* and eagle eye, we surmised a 6 iron would suffice. She hit a solid 6, which landed short of the green on the collar. Happy with par, she realized the 5 iron might have brought trouble with the two bunkers that flanked the green. We're happy, she's happy! Our job is done.

You always have the option of using or, if you feel another shot or club is a better option, disregarding our guidance. We don't get insulted. We fully understand and support all your choices, realizing it's a learning process—in all areas of life. The course helps you find *yourself* through golf.

During the fifth year of our relationship, since she has become more open and in sync with our guidance, we discovered that we can offer shot-selection advice. The first time we helped with shot selection, she had a sixty-yard shot and was planning to chip onto the green, due to winter conditions and a thin lie (a little grass under the ball, also called a tight lie). We guided her to use a pitching wedge. As she was standing over the ball, taking a practice stroke, she realized this wasn't enough club for the "chip and run" shot she'd imagined. We then zapped her intuitively, suggesting she take a full swing shot instead. She wasn't feeling confident with our recommendation, but then remembering who was on her bag, she said with conviction, "I am confident. I can do this!" After the ball landed on the green pin high, level with the flagstick, aghast, she thought, *since when are you helping me with shot selection?* Two holes later this happened again; Denise eagerly took our advice and hit a full shot instead of a chip. The wonders never cease!

It's thrilling to have this additional avenue of assistance available. With our wealth of know-it-all knowledge, we're unstoppable.

Just when Denise thought *what else could we possibly have up our wings*, we surprised her with a dandy. After pushing her drive, she was in the rough behind two pine trees. There was a wide enough gap for the long, low shot (stinger) we had orchestrated, and she felt confident with this plan. But as she took a couple of practice swings, she realized something about her stance was different from a typical stinger. For a moment she thought: *"Oh I should go back to my normal stance and swing for this type of shot,"* and then realized we were trying to tell her something. We instead had her use her pitching stance, using her five wood. Not what she was accustomed to. The shot blasted like a bullet, scurrying down the fairway. She realized a new trick *shot* was added to her bag.

Then there are those days of extreme golf conditions. We'll share what Denise has to say about that and the sink line and speed spots adjustments:

> The never-ending joy ride of golf ... twists and turns, hills and valleys, doglegs and aerated greens. Oh yes, today was the latter, with sandbox conditions ping-ponging the ball like an arcade machine, every which way but in. Also, adding firm fairways to the mix made for tests of all sorts. On the fourth hole, uphill par 3, my tee shot hit the first cut in front of the green and rolled thirty yards down the hill.

That made me realize golfers' flexibility isn't just about a full turn. It was going to be a round of patience, recovery, and boomerang golf.

Ricocheting circumstances made trusting the angels' assistance touchy. It also took acute awareness to identify the sink line and speed spot—like trying to find an emerald green ball marker. This called for drastic measures ... leaving it totally up to the angels and trusting their fall-in line was on target. To gauge the speed of the putt, their guidance on downhill putts was to use the actual hole for feel. And for uphill putts, to add 25 percent of the hole's distance. These harsh conditions led to many remarks, such as ... "Are you kidding me?" "What the heck? and "No way." It was a knee-knocking day.

Another day, after a perfectly struck second shot, Denise's ball rolled to the edge of a pond. The ground was very firm due to lack of rain, and her ball rolled further than planned. It was Adam Atomic, the Physicist Angel's day off ... just kidding! Actually, it was another valuable test we conjured up to reaffirm an important principle. In the past, if she hit a shot well and got an unfortunate result, she would be upset. So to make sure this was no longer the case, we threw a test her way.

As she walked toward the water's edge, she was relieved her ball didn't go into the pond. Since she used the club we recommended, as well as the target line, she was baffled as to why the ball was in such an awkward lie. With this stance, her feet were behind the ball, making for a challenging shot. Being overly impulsive and zealous to make this shot, she pulled the club we recommended but failed to discern the shot we were advising. You guessed it; the ball went into the water. Her predominant focus was to hit a one-in-a-million chip shot over the water, instead of conferring with us prior. To get her a sensible approach shot onto the green, our suggestion was to chip the ball sideways back into the fairway.

We realize that golf is a game of moving forward, but sometimes going sideways is the best *(and only)* option. When the ball is laterally passed in basketball, soccer, volleyball, or football, it is perfectly fine. So why do golfers frown upon this, when it may be the only optimal alternative? Is it embarrassing or despicable? There are no pictures on the scorecard, so we're puzzled.

This is a valuable lesson to take off the course. Taking that precious moment to be mindful and pause before acting is often by far the most valuable advice we can offer. Sometimes *going sideways* may serve as a metaphor for life, depicting a roundabout, scenic route or a not-as-planned path that may benefit in the long run. You'll never know what surprises await or what gifts we have up our wings if you take that heavenly detour.

We, however, do not advise moving the ball sideways in bowling—*alley hopping is glared upon*—even here in the angelic realm! Chess, anyone?

# P.A.R.
# Preshot Angel Routine

To get the ball rolling and enlist our services, a sincere call is needed, whether out loud, under your breath, or silently. This is best done before the round—possibly as you're getting ready, in the shower, having your coffee, or even driving to the course. It gives us time to get the monitors up and running, the situation scoped out, the assorted angels and fairies in position, and all of the cooperative components in place to orchestrate an outrageous outing for you.

Denise's pre-round call to us goes something like this ... "My angels, I give you the freedom to help me in every way to have fun, get fortuitous bounces, target alignment, club and shot selection, to clearly hear your guidance and easily see the signs you send," etc. Believe us; the list is extensive at times.

Your intentions may include that your ball fly

through the trees and skip through the bunkers with the greatest of ease, or you may even want nice flat lies with thick grass underneath. Or how about help with lining up your shots, advice on club selection, discerning the speed of the greens, or recommendations on shot selection? Did we miss anything? Add whatever your little heart desires to your request to make your round the most enjoyable ever.

Denise includes all of the aforementioned in her pre-round checklist. Since she realized her miracle account is unlimited, miracles are requested on just about every hole, for one reason or another. Your wish is our command. Dream big and believe! So with your intentions set, your laser focus, your A game, truckloads of trust, and your Angel Caddies on your bag, it's time to head to the course.

When you need a target line for your tee shot, stand behind the ball, imagine and visualize where you would like your ball to come to rest. Actually *see* the outcome with clarity. We'll provide the perfect target line for that to happen. As you stand behind your ball, look twenty to thirty feet in front for a spot that grabs your attention: possibly a leaf, old ball mark, or discoloration in the grass. This spot is your target line. You may also find it helpful to align the line on the ball with the target line. We've taken all the factors into consideration, including the most important one ... our *inside information*, which you're not privy to. Now it's time to address your ball with this target line and swing away with confidence.

There may be instances when the target line makes you uncomfortable and doesn't seem correct. When this occurs, we suggest you back off the ball. It is immensely important for you to feel confident and comfortable as you address the ball. Use discernment to determine whether it is a trust or a confidence issue. If your discomfort in addressing the ball is solely because of trusting the target line, make every attempt to believe with certainty and dig deep. As you gain faith in our collaboration, it will become easier and skepticism will diminish.

We'll also assist you with target lines on approach shots, pitch shots, and the putting green. When you request a target line, again look ahead of your ball for a spot or something that grabs your attention. It is extremely important not to overthink this and get the mind involved. This guidance comes quickly through your intuitive senses. Go with the first spot that snatches your attention, which may include any of the following:

leaf, discoloration in the grass, divot, goose poop, broken tee, pine cone, another player's ball.

Numerous times, after we provided Denise with a target line or a sink line, she received confirmation reaffirming the *spot* is correct. Another player's ball may have stopped on the target line, or perhaps the pin was pulled and laid on the green directly in line with the sink line. As her awareness increases, signs magically multiply.

The putting green is the true test for trust, both with us and you. Since you're already well versed with the *sink line* and *speed spot,* now the only thing required is your faith in the formula, which by all means is the defining factor in your success. There are numerous times (way too many to count!) that Denise would be standing over a two-foot putt, especially during a tournament, and mention the importance of this. We're passionately helping on every shot, every time, every round—*if that's your desire*—tournament or not, we're focused on the goal and the hole.

Okay, let's rehash! On the green, you have two viable options for our unwavering service. One is the sink line and the other the speed spot. First, line up your ball to the sink line, and then play a trick on your mind with the speed spot.

We'll delve and delude the mind in the next chapter, "Mind over Matter." Simply simple!

# Mind over Matter

Golf is the greatest game on Earth. It reaffirms the Divine has a sense of humor, and it challenges your mind, body, ego, and emotions. That's why we, the Golfing Angels, were commissioned to assist humanity with further enjoyment of the game. It wasn't until Denise called on us that we were put into service. Before that, we were sitting around, playing Asteroids from our Observation Deck. When we heard the call come in, we froze, thinking it a false alarm. But, not a nanosecond later, we all rushed to Denise to answer. We screamed with delight at the chance to help a human with the ups and downs of a game. Finally, we are inside the ropes! We are so grateful for the tons of patience it took Denise to teach us the rules. Since there are no rules where we are from, we fainted when we saw the USGA (U.S. Golf Association) *Rules of Golf*. It took a gaggle of fairies and a truckload of fairy dust to revive us! How can anything be fun with all those rules!

After study and observation, we easily saw that the biggest obstacle was the human mind. It always got in the way of the fun! We see you compare yourselves to others, and replay how you scored last week (whether high or low) on this hole or that, despite how we try to distract you. It was tough to get Denise to detach from her mind and ego, as both were very invested in the game —especially the score. In the early days, she rarely seemed satisfied with a shot, even if the outcomes were perfectly acceptable. Even *with* good shots, we felt Denise's undercurrent of dissatisfaction. Now that *we* are on her bag, she is a new person! Her transformation on (and off!) the course has been so dramatic that we hardly recognize her! She no longer beats herself up over shots, and if something isn't hit quite the way she planned, she knows that all is well, and that we'll help her execute the next shot with precision.

Recently in a four-person team event, she hit five truly ugly shots during the round, but the results turned out according to her intention, as if she hit the shots well. Intrigued by this, she asked how it happened. It's understandable for one or perchance two shots. But five? We explained that with her intense focus, intention, and visualization, the Universe provided the outcome she was expecting, even though the shots weren't well struck. Reminding her that deliberate goal setting is more important than the sweet spot. And if you're wondering if we were involved in the antics and orchestration, the answer is an astounding yes.

We suggested the game should be named "Recovery," since that's what you must do most of the time, anyway! Denise's joy for the game is overflowing, and we've had to replace the fun-ometer a dozen times, since she keeps turning up the volume into the red zone and shorts it out! What a quality problem to have.

Denise realized that if she keeps her emotions as even as a glassy lake, any internal turmoil in a game won't faze her at all. We've coached her to find the positive, beneficial aspects in every scenario, detaching (as much as humanly possible) from the outcome. The true game is either lost or won between the mind-emotion connection, and blending the two into harmony and balance. Rising up above the ego mind takes commitment and perseverance, but is the ultimate victory if you want to claim freedom.

Recently during a team tournament, Denise

found it nearly impossible to hear or communicate with us. When she asked for target lines, they never seemed correct; her confidence waned, adding anxiety. The greens were so slick that even putting felt like a comical circus for the team. Putts zoomed past their holes and lipped out left and right, and then she decided to accept the conditions, realizing that every other team had the same course to play. Her angel connection was never really lost, but on every tee box she focused to "regain" it. Trying too hard only further contributed to the feeling of being unplugged from us—which was not the case!

We think it's necessary to share Denise's blow by blow to give you a realistic view of how things sometimes are. It's not all peaches and cream!

From Denise's journal:

> Yesterday on the second hole, I focused and intended my drive to be left fairway and I wound up in the right rough. And not just rough; my ball was in a low spot and my stance was above the ball on an uphill lie. I was able to chop it out and move it forward forty yards. This seemed to be the theme of the day. Just missing putts by a hair and my ball ending up in wild and crazy places, where I've never

> been before. I told my partners, "I've never been here on the course. I'm getting my money's worth." But I thought: *What's the deal? I was utilizing the angels' help, so why all the trouble?* In hindsight, I may have been trying too hard, which gives my ego full reign and disconnects me from the angels, instead of allowing enjoyment of each shot to be my prime concern. This sometimes happens when I want to impress others or really score well, like in a tournament. It also severed me from my fun self and made me way too serious, which tensed up my body. The angels definitely don't like that and neither does my spirit.

Even after years of working with us, this can happen. Our recommendation is: If you don't feel the connection, don't worry. Relax, for we are always working diligently and answering all of your requests and needs. Trying too hard and struggling brings in stress and negative energy, which only makes your experience worse. When you bring tension in, your sixth sense—the one where you notice our nudges—temporarily shorts out. And, really, you never know; when circumstances don't appear as planned, remember that somehow, we have a surprise up our wings.

In addition to stress and strain, our connection may wane when it rains. As rain enveloped the course, it proved to be a soggy start to the two-day Member-Member tournament. Denise was sporting rain gear from head to toe, with ten towels in tow and eight spare gloves. By the last four holes, the foursome was squishy and their grips were squashy, making it impossible to hold on to the club. "Cart path only" rule meant our shots were furthest from the path intentionally producing additional exposure to the elements. The majority of her energy was on maintaining dry grips and keeping up with superfluous supply of towels and gloves ... not an easy task. A real-life caddie would have come in handy!

This additional exertion depleted her energy and diminished the (perceived) flow of guidance. Although she unceasingly called forth assistance for target lines, club selection, and reading the soppy greens, with dampened focus it became challenging to hear. Our usual coaching, rooting, motivating, and cheering techniques with pom-poms were not easily sensed. We even turned up the volume on our messages and hooked up boom boxes to clarify the communication—*imagination is everything!*

Sometimes our communication diminishes because of other factors. When the temperature soars into the 100 degree range, so does Denise's game! For instance, one day the sizzling heat clouded her ability to hear us, and her game started with a drive off the first tee going left and out of bounds. On the next hole, she lost her ball on the approach shot; just when a tree fairy yawned before her afternoon nap, she accidentally swallowed it! Even when Denise called out to us countless times for a miracle, the search-and-rescue mission was unsuccessful, due to the fairy's indigestion. Denise —rather uncharacteristically—lost four balls in the first six holes. And even though she connected with us about her wishes and dreams for the game and meditated and stretched in preparation, it became impossible for her to hear us and discern our help that day. Even when she asked for the volume to be turned up on our communication, we watched in disappointment that even our megaphones didn't help. Despite our cheering, coaching, and collaborating, the extreme heat closed down the creative part of her mind, where the connection to us is curated. Because it isn't necessary for survival, blood flow to this part of the brain diminished to keep the rest of her in balance. Everyone in the foursome had similar difficulties, and rightfully so. Our recommendations: bring an umbrella to shade yourself on the green, a cold towel for the back of your neck, buckets of ice to cool down your water and your core temperature, or stay indoors on hot days! That's what the golf channel is for!

Even a seasoned angel golfer has rounds that aren't always, in each and every moment, joyful. But we remind Denise (and you as well) that feeling struggle or disconnection can often simply be an opportunity to slow down and re-center, since we are never *truly* disconnected.

# There's Always Hope

The dictionary meaning of hope is the expectation and desire for a certain thing to happen. Hope for a human is way more important than imagined. Without it you succumb to dingy energy and dismay. Denying your power comes with difficult days on the course. Hope is available to all, free of charge; it only takes a slight shift in mental focus to release those unwanted old programs. Humans may think it's easier *to give up* and by doing so believe they remove themselves of responsibility from the situation and are free, when in fact it's the opposite. Hope brings in positive, uplifting energy. That in turn will assist in claiming your power to amend and rectify a situation, bringing in good vibes, exhilaration and happiness, and possibly a one putt. Chip, chip away!

This was a long and tedious lesson for Denise to learn and relearn. If things didn't go her way, she was in the habit of giving up, blaming a long list of external factors, like the blue sky, unfair bounces, a bad hair day, an annoying playing partner, the wind, etc. This was an obsolete habit with no positive attributes. It had been an ongoing process for some time until one day she realized we were working diligently on every shot and giving up was negating our efforts. Recognizing this, she needed to be responsible. Not sink into victim consciousness and hopelessness, succumbing to negative thoughts. With this new attitude, she became determined and realized the potential in each shot in every moment.

When she focused on the shot in front of her with full attention and brought her awareness to the now, she strongly experienced and entirely embraced empowerment and finally fully felt its influence. It made her realize that in the past she habitually gave up her power and enjoyment of the moment. Once this understanding took a firm hold, things dramatically shifted. When in the past an errant drive would have caused her to score a triple bogey, she now digs in deep on all cylinders and musters up fierce focus to stay even-keeled and positive. She can hole out from anywhere and realizes that's a possibility. Releasing this old behavior has exponentially increased her fun and lowered her golf score too. Imagine that!

When Denise found herself in a ravine left of the fairway on her second shot on a par 5, with her ball in a clump of stuff and a rock behind it, she thought: *What the heck am I doing here? ... I hit a good shot ... Is this a test?* So instead of regressing into the obsolete thoughts of giving up, she dug deep and chopped down on the ball with a 9 iron, moving it thirty yards forward to the second cut of the green. Luckily, she missed the rock (yes, we were overseeing that), and her club and hand were unscathed.

This was during a close match in a team tournament, so the pressure was on. After chipping up onto the green, her ball was twenty-five feet from the hole. When we showed her the line, she questioned it, thinking it was too far to the right. After conferring, she accepted the target and hit it with authority, and woohoo ... in the hole for par!

If Denise had thrown in the towel, she would have brought in low vibes. Instead, with her positive thoughts and a just-do-it attitude, we were available to orchestrate this outrageous occurrence. This brought reassurance that to focus on positivity, with trust and faith, means anything is possible. As these experiences occur, she's gaining confidence in us and herself and getting stronger to permanently release the "poor is me" syndrome. Alleluia!

In another two-person team event Denise was just short of the green in 2 on a par 4. Her partner was on the green in regulation. So we gave Denise an aggressive line for her chip shot, which came to rest twenty feet from the hole. Thinking she was out of the hole, since her partner would either birdie or par, Denise was relaxed. Her partner putted first and left it short. Denise's putt had a five-foot break and found the center cut for par. Her partner missed the par putt, so Denise's result counted for the net score on the hole. Her high expectations and belief that something good might happen allowed us to manifest this. Expect with absolute faith, trust, and conviction in the promise that anything is possible. It's not over till it's over!

Here is an experience Denise wanted to share ...

> As I was putting for birdie a few holes later, my putt hit an old ball mark—bump in the road —and was thrown ever so slightly off course. The tap-in par was fine, although there was an ounce of disappointment, especially since I was on the green in regulation and had a birdie putt. It felt like a lost opportunity. On the very next hole, my drive landed in the right rough,

the second shot went in the bunker in front of the green, third shot five feet from the hole, fourth shot in the hole for par, which was oh so gratifying. I realized, after examining these two back-to-back pars, the angels had yet another lesson up their wings. The first par was nice and easy, but the second was much more rewarding, fulfilling, and all around fun—as I was able to squeak out a par with so many obstacles in my path. This made me realize, sometimes we are thrown off course by a bump in the road, which could be discouraging. Taking the scenic route—bypassing the fairway—encouraged me to focus and hone in. These challenges and hurdles strengthened my conviction and demonstrated the end results can be the same with focus on the goal ... or the hole.

We see humans give up so easily at times, without a battle. Often you must knuckle down to find an inner core of strength you never knew you had and muster up the courage to continue when all hope seems gone. To transcend all old beliefs and outdated ways of thinking and behaving is immensely important in your evolution.

Your power lies within you—*in the now*—and

you must dig deep to discover this valuable treasure.
So well worth the excavation!

# Surrender

Remember as a kid, you would tickle your friends until they screamed, "I surrender!" Well, it's like that. The Universe places in your path many things for soul's growth that force you to stop and surrender, or suffer. All is good! When we told Denise this, she scratched her head in dismay. Once she realized the logic, accepting the present moment and circumstances, she relinquished the ego's control and peace would prevail. We're fascinated by the human mind and its evolution and get great satisfaction in the strides she has attained. With wonder and amazement we cheer her on.

One day when the greens were slick and superfast and her putts were lipping out, we informed her ... "Sometimes it rains, and if you resist it, it only makes it worse." The slippery-slick greens persisted for over a month, so our two-cents came in handy and helped in the surrendering process.

There is no one, singular exercise to encourage a golfer to surrender other than practicing acceptance, but we angels know that the point of any sport is to embrace joy for the inner child, so our suggestion is to see the surrender point as a moment to let the Universe take back the reins, and to take a deep breath to relax.

When resistance to what was happening occurred, it brought in stress and strain, and as you can imagine, it hindered her naturally flowing swing. This routine of resisting the present moment with dread, instead of accepting it with empowerment, was the norm. It took years to eliminate this old tendency. It occurred mostly on days when she was striking the ball well and wasn't scoring low, or when she got unfavorable bounces and with unacceptance and minor complaining brought in more of the same stuff. When you complain, you make yourself a victim and bad vibes reverberate in your being. So there!

We had a gaggle full of giggles this one day on the fourteenth hole. Denise pulled her drive to the left and hit a few trees, landing in the fairway of the fifteenth hole. You're probably wondering why the ball didn't land in her fairway, since we're on the job. Well, we do put Denise through tests; we can't resist a good one now and then. As she's becoming a master over the material in this book, our testing opportunities are more infrequent. Her request to us before her round during her P.A.R. (preshot angel routine) was for fortuitous bounces and for her ball to land in the fairway. She didn't exactly specify *which* fairway. You see, you do need to be very specific with us; otherwise, we do take our liberties occasionally, just for frivolity. So getting back to the matter at hand, we recommended she hit the second shot down the fifteenth fairway, as there was no opportunity through the trees to get back to the fourteenth fairway. That left her 150 yards out of light rough to the hole. With full surrender to the conditions and acceptance of what was, the test was complete. Since she maintained a calm demeanor, she was easily able to receive clear guidance on club and shot selection. This then gave us the ability to merrily manifest miracles.

On the 150-yard shot, she intended for the ball to land on the green. The ball came out like a rocket, a little left of the green, jumped through the bunker—doing a twirl in the air—and landed on the first cut just off the green, forty feet from the hole. The other ladies in the group remarked on the flair of the shot; we were delighted. With a chip and two-putt, marking a bogey on the card, she was pleased with the outcome, grateful for the unorthodox way to play the hole with grace and ease. Voilà!

We again mastered a dramatic dance on the next hole, as the approach shot ricocheted off the sides of the bunker and dove out onto a patch of grass in between two bunkers. The other players commented they never saw anything like that. She knew unquestionably we were diligently mustering the many magical moments. Surrender allows serendipities to spring forth.

Another lesson surfaced during the round as she was standing over a thirty-foot putt. Here are the details from Denise:

> The sink line the angels provided—*straight*—just didn't seem right. There was shade and sun mixed all through the sink line, which created an illusion. To my eye, it seemed the putt would break hard right. As I pondered this dilemma, I went with my decision and three putted. Trust is a tricky thing. Just when I feel I've mastered the trust thing, the angels throw an illusion my way. As the ball turns, so does this—another metaphor mirroring my life—reminding me the angels are always supporting me, even if there

> is a delusion staring me in the face. It can be difficult to take your hands off the wheel—a scary thing. As my trust grows in teeny matters, I gain more confidence and faith in the colossal ones too ... like club selection ... now we're talking spine-chilling!

Denise had the opportunity to play a team event with a local ladies' league at another course. And, of course, we brought enlightenment to her round. Here's the recap:

> As I was standing on the twelfth tee, looking at the landscape before me, it became evident I had no clarity on what club to hit. I was playing this course for the first time, hence the confusion. Before I called on the angels, a fellow player, a member from this course, remarked, "It's a lay-up about 150 yards." I continued to gaze down the fairway, trying to put the topography into perspective. Were my eyes deceiving me? It seemed so much further. If the drive wasn't long enough, the second shot would have to carry over a pond to a severely elevated green flanked by a stone wall. It made for a very intimidating hole.

When I *finally* consulted with the angels, a 7 wood was their recommendation. I knew with full trust this was the correct club, but with tenseness in my body and anxiety about the unnerving hole, I pulled the shot left into a fairway bunker. Undeniably, trying to get everything out of the club, I over swung. My next shot was short—a lay-up—that splashed into the pond and led to a triple bogey.

This perplexing perspective made me ponder. From the tee box the hole was daunting, but as played, it became evident it wasn't as menacing as first perceived. All that was needed was a halfway decent tee shot in the fairway, which would then reveal with more certainty what was needed for the next shot and so on. By dissecting the hole piece by piece, it became feasible. Golf course architects are obligated to create illusions with elevation changes, bunkers, and water features to keep us second-guessing, and they certainly got me on this one. I can still hear them laughing!

I realized that playing through this hole was an analogy for my life. Looking at the finish (of a project, golf hole, or dream) is overwhelming and could create stress and apprehension—or even the F word ... *fear!* But taking one shot at a time, surrendering, and enlisting the angels to navigate the terrain, keeps it fun, on target, and transforms the perceived challenges into illusions. Oh, the confusing delusions of the mind!

We gently remind you that your full power lies in the now. By getting too far ahead of yourself and worrying about the outcome, you'll diminish your creativity and our connection. Instead, we recommend visualizing the hole like a road map, plotting your course from point A to point B, and only focusing on that segment of the trip. The journey will unfold with twists and turns, doglegs and rotations, bringing you to your desired destination, embracing enthusiasm instead of dread. Golf's a course, not a destination.

# Scrap the Score

Yes, we certainly understand you wish to play well, but playing well and stressing about your score are not related. As silly as this may sound, the score is the least important aspect of your round. We know you find your score a significant part of the game, as a way of charting your progress and comparison. We find humor in how you gauge your enjoyment of golf, with a pencil. It's all about the score, rather than enjoying an extraordinary shot you may have executed out of the bunker or possibly one of your longest drives. Judging yesterday's round by tomorrow's is nonsensical too, since there is no way to adequately compare—that was that and this is this. Every moment is different—from the weather to your physiology—on any given day. How well you played should not be determined by a number at the end of your round, instead of by your quotient of joy, exhilaration, relaxation, laughter, magical moments, sunshine, fresh air, nature, comradery, and achievements. Golf should be played for the sheer pleasure of it—grinding is optional.

Scrapping the score and focusing on fun, hole by hole, is mastery. It takes keen attention and intention to bring the power that lies in the moment into awareness. The most creative sticks in the bag are your clubs, not the pencil. The wealth of imagination you can muster from fourteen clubs is astounding—each one providing an array of options to devise a stupendous shot. Our advice is to embrace enjoyment first and foremost, for that will accelerate the plummeting of your handicap. It's best to remove and release all emotional charges from the score. It will take some practice, since for most people this has become an ingrained habit. But it will afford freedom to your mind and a fluid, unencumbered motion to your body. Worry restricts the flow of good vibes and brings in the shanks, yips, yanks, and possibly even a chili dip—and we don't mean at the turn!

It's most enjoyable for us to witness when Denise is playing a team event, like a Captain's Choice tournament, where her score isn't relevant. There is more lightness and joy in her step, knowing that importance is on the team score, not her individual tally. It's fun to see each member work together toward a common goal and cheer each other to greatness. It's not often that golf is a team event; it's always a nice change of pace from the "me against you for a quarter a hole" mentality. With this lightness, Denise tends to play her best, relinquishing her competitive edge, fully present to buoy her fellow players' spirit.

She realized this was the case many years ago and worked to detach from her score, as much as humanly possible. Her transformation is incredible. Going with the flow is her mantra, and having the most fun in each moment while being fully present, pretty much sums it up nicely. Well, that is true the majority of the time. When she hit the green in regulation, on a hole she hadn't been on in a while, she was thrilled and thought: *I have par or better.* Well, you know what happened next ... she three putted. Need we say more? As she walked off the green, she realized what happened. Her mind got ahead, with focus on the possible score instead of the now. It's a learning process. Two steps forward, one back. Oh, the *lengths* we go to!

Here's a day that didn't go as planned, as told by Denise:

As I was walking the course, in a *detached*

*from the score* mode, *in the flow, zoned out* kind of place, a fellow player asked what I shot on the front. It's the sixteenth hole when she asked, and all I could think was: *Am I playing that well?* It was a relaxing round, with very few hiccups. So when this question entered my awareness, I started to think about my score and if I was having a personal best or close to it.

On my way to the seventeenth hole, a bit of apprehension came into my consciousness. If I were having a really good scoring round, I better not blow it and play safe. This, of course, is fear in a low vibration, and it will only play havoc with your game and focus if you let it in. Needless to say, I did (let it in), and my going with the flow, focus on fun was smothered, which contributed to a double bogey on the last two holes.

When my awareness shifted to the outcome instead of living in the moment, my concentration was choked, and I failed to determine if the putts were uphill or down, causing both to lip out. I knew the angels were reaffirming a valuable lesson, especially when I saw one of the chapters—*Scrap the Score*—in my mind's eye. In hindsight, I realize my playing partner's question was out of character, and therefore, had to have been orchestrated by the angels to wallop me out of my old ways, yet again.

I take full responsibility for giving the end result greater prominence than extracting pure pleasure from each shot. I could have easily chosen to go about my round in the usual fashion, oblivious of the outcome. The metaphoric message may possibly be not to be sidetracked by others or outside influence and to remain detached, deliberately determined, and downright zoomed in.

I realize detaching from the outcome gives the angels full liberty to fill in the blanks, without my mind hindering the results, providing amazing synchronicities and maybe even a hole-in-one. I'm learning to leave room for a plethora of possibilities.

Oh, you're going to love this, 'cause we did. Denise just finished writing this chapter. The next day when she played, we had her live it fully, along with all the other chapters. Talk about euphoria! With "Scrap the Score" fresh in mind, we had her parring many holes, except for those where the putt rolled over the edge … keeping her humble. She completed the front nine with an exceptional score of 38. Even though she didn't add up her score, she knew that—with three bogeys on her card—she was 3 over par. It was challenging at times to remain detached from the score and not get ahead of herself.

The one thing that helped distract her was a talkative playing companion, keeping her oblivious to her running tally. We also threw in a tad of surrendering to the moment, maintaining hope, accepting what is, and being mindful of her thoughts, to thoroughly test her adeptness. She's getting the hang of it and we are confident you will too!

Here are some additional insightful insights into score which we'll let Denise share, involving her personal transformation:

> Walking the course and feeling the Earth under my feet is magical. I felt incredibly relaxed and more present than ever, giving each shot my full attention and executing with conviction. This made the round fun, while I was also being diligent about detaching from the score. Before

the angels were on my bag, I would use a lot of effort to make things happen and golf became work. If my drive didn't find the fairway, I would give up on the hole before leaving the tee box, winding up with a double or triple bogey. I was very attached to the score, and the outcome was more important than enjoying each shot. Now as soon as I catch myself thinking about score or adding up the score on a hole before it's over, I pull my awareness back, usually by thinking about something totally irrelevant. Golf, being a game of recovery, warrants flexibility with the circumstances and awareness of self. My old, obsolete give-up self has transformed and a genuine metamorphosis has occurred. It's amusing to reminisce, as well as embarrassing too.

Recently in a tournament, Denise played in a foursome with a man who took an extraordinary amount of time over each shot. It was tedious, draining, exhausting, and extremely time-consuming. Was he having a good time? It certainly didn't appear so. Stress puts pressure on your body, which will permeate your swing if you're not conscious of it.

Scrapping the score has another benefit, by keeping your mind in the now—not letting it race ahead to what will happen if you do this, that, and the other thing on the next hole or what you shoulda-coulda done in the past. It's a given that you and all golfers wish to score low every round. We recommend focusing on playing well by executing the best shot you can each and every time confidently. When you're connected—*to us and Creator*—your intuition and inspiration is the most valuable source of guidance. Go with your first instinct and you will succeed.

Removing fret and anxiety from your round is freeing, allowing us to shower you with magical moments and lucky breaks beyond your wildest dreams. When you try too hard (fear in disguise), it diminishes our lines of communication. We'll certainly try to lighten you up with our array of tricks we have up our wings. We won't share these with you now, since we want you to be surprised when it happens. Can we get a piñata for the fifth hole?

# Dress for Show Putt for Dough

We found it's not just about hitting the sweet spot; it's about looking sharp too. Looking snazzy and feeling good is uplifting and helps instill a favorable frame of mind. It breeds an air of confidence and self-assurance.

We immensely enjoy Denise's preplanning for team events. There are many decisions: choosing a team color, name, song, and many times golf cart decoration too, especially for holiday tournaments like Easter, July 4th, Halloween, or New Year's Day. All these things help congeal the team and bring in positive uplifting energy.

It's especially fun when she plays with a friend twice a year in a Member-Member two-day event. They go all out by getting matching outfits from visor to socks. In addition to solidifying their bond, they intimidate the field by looking like they're on a winning mission, serious about this tournament thing. Their main focus is on the fun thing, but ... shhhh ... don't tell the field!

One morning before the first day's event, Denise asked us for a motivating song for her and her teammate. She asked us to—when she turned on Pandora—pick the song for that day's round. The song we chose for day one was "Shake Your Groove Thing" and for the second day "Ain't No Stopping Us Now." Now and then throughout their round, they would sing the song to stay on track, congeal their bond, or for a chuckle. We were quite delighted to be called on for song choice (there's a first for everything) and thought we did a splendid job. We did, however, consult with Marvin the Motivational Music Angel for recommendations. The sky's the limit to our talents, so ask away, 'cause ain't no stopping us now ... we're in the groove!

Now that you're *dressed* for show, it's time to putt for dough. We all know tournaments are won on the putting green, so keep the requests coming full throttle. Putting Angel Pete is willing and able to assist with the speed spot and sink line; don't hesitate to call for his assistance anytime, any green.

During a recent tournament an amusing thing happened when Denise called in Putting Angel Pete. She sunk (yes for real ... we have testimonials) a ninety-foot putt for birdie—told her foursome about the help she solicits from the angelic realm. She mentioned Pete's name and they all perked up, their eyes wide and their faces priceless as they processed this data. With her seriousness on the subject, they didn't know whether to laugh or dismiss her confidences as rubbish. We love it when humans hear about us for the first time.

It's now the ninth hole and she has another long putt. One of the ladies on the opposing team said, "Denise, this putt is in your wheelhouse." Missing it by a fraction, Denise said, "For Pete's sake!" totally by accident, and they all burst into laughter. You just can't make this stuff up.

During team events, when a plethora of information is readily shared regarding yardage, speed of the greens, and putting line (just to mention a few!), with all the outside advice it may become more difficult to hear us. It's like your expression ... TMI. Once during a team event at an away course, one of the team members played there weekly; the others, including Denise, had not. Therefore, there was much information to divulge, especially about the target lines for tee shots and putting green speed and break, which made it utterly impossible to hear our words of wisdom and discern what would be the best action.

The good news is that realizing this, she was able to somewhat, as best she could, detach from the data being exchanged. The Bermuda greens were very tricky; they played lightning fast downhill and Velcro slow uphill. As this type of grass is different from the team's home course, it challenged the foursome, and as each tried to help, it may have actually hindered. With the disparity between the downhill and uphill putting speed, it certainly played mind games and was hampering each player's feel.

Even with coordinating team colors and decorated golf carts, the uncertain green speed diminished their confidence. It turned out to be a good learning experience for Denise when placed in this situation. Work in progress!

# The Nineteenth Hole

On the morning of the annual Ladies' League Holiday Luncheon, Denise asked us for material for the book. Even though she wasn't playing golf, she figured anything was possible. Little did she know we had already concocted a plan, which we had been working on during the year, to give her tangible proof of our immense impact on her game. We knew this would be a wonderful holiday gift and were eagerly awaiting the surprise.

The Ladies' League has a *birdie tree* located in the clubhouse; every time you make a birdie, you place a paper birdie on this tree, with your name, date, and hole number. We were so excited when it was announced that Denise had the most birdies in the league for the year. By a landslide, we might add. We knew she would be delighted to have palpable printed proof on a spreadsheet. She thanked us profusely, and we weren't sure (at first) if she was more delighted with having the most birdies or with concrete material for the book. We believe it's the latter.

The league also has a ringer card for each participant's best score at that golf course for each hole, which is updated every time a better score is achieved on a particular hole. She again was squealing with delight, this time at achieving first place in her flight, yet again adding tangible proof. For this performance, she even won some loot. Although the money was nice, the confirmation and proof made her beam with gratitude and gave her perfect closure for the book.

Being the test dummy since 2010 wasn't always easy. In order to acquire first-hand material for the book and solidify the process, we needed a surrogate. At times, she had to get banged around, to define the lines of communication and develop a clear plan of execution. Not included in *Golfing with the Angels* are hundreds of stories of her trials and tribulations. We'll let her share those with you as she makes her rounds—on and off the course—throughout the world, and in future books.

Along the journey, she grew immensely as a person and learned valuable lessons. Although at first, she thought writing this book was just a journal for her, soon she realized it was a gift that had to be shared to benefit all. As Denise sits here, writing these words for us, she is eagerly anticipating the time when she can play a round, with us in tow, with no more material to obtain and experience. Little does she know the journey has just begun. What fun we'll have, navigating the terrain, on her bag until eternity or the nineteenth hole, whichever comes first.

The guidance from all of us angels is as simple and complex as life: ask for and trust the Divine help you get, have fun, and be courageous when you're called to do something important. That's the point of it all, anyway.

Ain't nothing stopping us now, we're on a roll! Who's that singing off-key ... is that you, Pete?

# Golf Lingo Glossary

***ball mark***

blemish made by an incoming ball onto the green

***bunkers***

sand trap

***center cut***

ball drops into hole without touching the sides

***collar***

where the fringe meets the putting green

***dogleg***

curve in the fairway mimicking a dog's leg

***dry grips***

hands on the club free of moisture

***five footer***

five-foot putt to the hole

**five-*foot break***

putt will curve five feet due to slope on the green

***fringe***
closely mowed area around the green

***full turn***
body rotation in the golf swing

***green in regulation***
ball reaches the green in two strokes less than par

***lay-up***
opt to land the ball short of the green

***line on the ball***
line drawn on the ball for alignment purposes

***lipped out***
ball hits the lip of the hole and ricochets out

***pin***
flagstick standing in the cup (hole) on the green

***pin high***
ball stops in alignment with the flagstick

***stinger***
low trajectory shot with significant roll

***tap-in***
a putt so short it is guaranteed to go in

***through the break***
putting firmly lessening the curve on the green

# Epilogue

Standing on the tee box of a 120-yard par 3 with the wind steadily blowing into my face, I understood the need to hit more club and keep the shot low. The angels heard my request, suggesting I use my hybrid. After watching a fellow player's ball get swept up into the wind and pushed into a bunker, I agreed with the angels' club selection.

As I prepared to address the ball, I saw in my mind's eye the ball cutting through the wind and landing pin high. Well, needless to say, the angels had a far more unconventional outcome up their wings. I hit the ball thin, it rolled *on the ground* for 120 yards, through thick grass, down a hill, and up another, finally settling on the back of the green. Certainly, the longest putt I've ever hit—with a hybrid, no less! What about physics?

In hindsight, the message ... *and there's always one!* ... is not to be concerned with the dreaded hows. The angels, the Universe, God—whichever force resonates—orchestrated the most outrageous outcome in alignment with my request. It just wasn't what I visualized or how I thought it would happen, but the end result materialized with remarkable precision.

This demonstration served as a metaphor for my daily life, offering me greater freedom as I ask, plead, and command their help on an array of things, from parking spots to publishing this book.

With daily intention and focus on my dreams and goals, and with their unwavering support, my desires will manifest—perhaps not as planned, but nonetheless, as dramatic and fulfilling beyond what my mind can conceive. It's all in the request!

# Afterword

*It's not about being perfect.*

*It's about making the best out of*

*every situation ... and lie.*

# Acknowledgement

Diana Henderson for *literally* getting the ball rolling when I mentioned I'm enlisting the angels help on the golf course to which she enthusiastically replied, "You need to write a book." To which I emphatically replied, "No, I don't think so."

Lizzie Appel was the *first* to read the manuscript, which shook me to the bones as I hit the send button. It was an eye-opening experience as we crafted the book proposal with imagination and joy.

Margaret A. Harrell wholeheartedly embraced the concept and my vision, and was willing to joyfully edit *with* the golfing angels, under their supervision of course. An enlightening, enjoyable and expansive experience for sure.

My mom, Joan Kane, who continues to be a driving force in my life. With her *keen* eye for detail, I feel her working through me from beyond. Sharing her humor, giving me a leg up, as well as providing courage and confidence as I explore new horizons, always rooting me on my way.

# About The Author

## Denise Kane

Denise is an avid tournament golfer, author, artist, and Reiki Master/Teacher practitioner.

Butterfly Reiki, her healing center, where she offers client sessions, Reiki certifications, and teaches her unique Violet Flame Workshop, inspired by her book, "The Violet Flame: A Game Changer!" available on Amazon (link below).

The fluid art paintings she creates are channeled energy transmissions of Light frequency, designed to restore health and well-being and enhance prayer and meditation sessions. These "Paintings with Soul to Make you Whole" can be found at her Etsy Shop (link below).

She established the Violet Stars Lightworkers group in 2015, which still conducts weekly Sunday prayer calls. Recordings of these sessions are available on her YouTube channel.

Additional humorous anecdotes, as she rolls with the Golfing Angels, may be found on her Blog (link below).

During her thirty-eight-year career with American Airlines, Denise knew there had to be more to life than changing passengers' seat assignments and getting planes to depart on time. In 2006 she "woke up," which opened the door to the world of angels, transforming her views.

She had been a corporate employee; now, in little more than the blink of an eye, she finds herself firmly on a different path, determined to play her role in bringing the angels and the violet flame to heal the world.

Website: www.denisekane.com

YouTube: www.youtube.com/denisekane

Etsy: EnergyFlowPaintings.Etsy.com

Amazon: https://bit.ly/3W2sDwk (Violet Flame)

Blog: www.angels4golf.com

# Books By This Author

## The Violet Flame: A Game Changer!

Ready to let go of what's holding you back and release what no longer serves you?

This book introduces the Violet Flame—a simple yet powerful daily practice for clearing stress, emotional pain, and limiting beliefs. Through focused intention and inspired affirmations, you'll learn how to transmute heavy energy into clarity, balance, and renewed strength, creating lasting postive change.

Featuring forty-six original decrees and clear, step-by-step guidance, this book supports deep healing, personal growth, and a more abundant, empowered life—all in as little as fifteen minutes a day.

Step into a lighter, brighter way of living. Reconnect with your true potential, reclaim your power, and begin transforming your inner world—starting now.

www.ingramcontent.com/pod-product-compliance
Lightning Source LLC
La Vergne TN
LVHW090614110826
845146LV00001B/387

* 9 7 9 8 9 9 9 1 9 7 2 0 7 *